The Book of Breath Prayers:

A *Faith-ing Project* Guide

by

Jeff Campbell

For more information on contemplative practices, or to contact the author, go to https://faithingproject.com/

No table of contents entries found.

Introduction

There are many things being said about meditation, contemplation, and prayer. It would be hard to not know about the proven benefits of mindfulness and related practices.
Once a person decides they want to begin down this path things begin to get complicated. It seems like everybody has a different idea about how to do these things. It is a bit like pizza. If you had never had a pizza before, lots of people would be willing to tell you which pizza is the best pizza. Generally speaking, it would probably be the pizza that they are making.

It is true that there are some objectively bad pizzas. Similarly, there are some contemplative practices which are not particularly helpful most everyone. But more often, it is about finding a good match. Deep dish pizzas are not inherently better than thin crust. Yet, certain people will believe them to be so. Correspondingly, there are some practices which are simply a better match for this person or that person.

If you knew nothing about pizza, it would be a bit of a task to have to travel to all the pizza places to explore them. If you were interested in such a quest, it would certainly simplify things if someone would bring all the pizza together so that you could try it one place.

Metaphorically speaking, this is the mission of *The Faith-ing Project*. We seek to aid you in building your spiritual practice by assembling a diverse group of contemplative practices for you to consider. This is done through the website https://faithingproject.com/ , through monthly email explorations, and through ebooks such as the one you are currently holding.

There are many wonderful books which take a deep exploration into the theory of how and why meditation works. There are numerous explorations of religious doctrine. This book will not attempt to cover that important ground.

What this book will do is present you with several exercises you can begin today. There is some background information for these exercises, and step-by-step instructions. As you might have inferred from the title, these practices rely heavily on the breath. Many of these practices and much of my language is rather Christian-oriented. This is not meant to diminish the importance of any other faith tradition. It is simply where I am coming from. (Just as the fact that this book is being written in English does not imply that English is better than any other language. It is simply indicates some biographical facts about where I come.)

If you commit to 15-30 minutes each day, I believe that you will see real changes in your life. People find that contemplation builds a sense of calm and joy in their lives. You might spend a single day on each exercise in this book and cycle through all of them over the next two-and-a-half weeks.

You also could read through all of them and cherry pick the ones that seem like good places to start. Or maybe you will stick with an exercise for several days, and move on to the next when you are ready.

Many of the exercises in this book are available as audiofiles. You can find them at https://faithingproject.com/audio-files-associated-with-publications-of-the-faith-ing-project/

It might be that the exercises here are enough to build your spiritual practice for the foreseeable future. Or maybe this book is just a launching pad into a deeper exploration of other practices. The website listed above, and future *Faith-ing Project* e-books will be one set of resources you might use.

Much like life, there are many ways to do this well.

I believe that in the long run, it will be best for you to settle in to just a few exercises. Over the long term, this seems to be where the spiritual growth happens. But there is a world of practices out there! So let's begin.

Section 1: I am breathing

There seems to be no statement more self evident than this: I am breathing.

And so, this is a good place to begin: with the assumption that I am breathing. On the pages that follow, you will find 14 exercises that begin with precisely this assumption.

Following these 14 breath prayers are a pair of exercises which belong to the cateogry of sacred reading. More specifically, these are *Lectio Divina* practices. They are included in this book because they help to give a way of understanding the scriptutre used in some of these earlier exercises.

Following exercise 16, you will find section 2. Section 2 turns this assumption-- that I am breathing-- on its head. These ending exercises may be useful to you. It is, of course, useful to question our assumptions.

At the same time, it is also useful to begin at the beginning. So let us begin here, at the beginning: I am breathing.

Exercise #1: God's Name

Background

There is a long history, in the Jewish Tradition, around the saying of God's name. It might have begun with Moses, being told by a burning bush that the name of God was a word which we often render into English as Yahweh. If you would like to take a deep dive into this bible passage, turn to exercise number 16.

In the centuries that followed, there was often resistance to saying God's name. Christianity inherited that tradition in the use of the word "LORD" for God: all in small capital letters.

Some Rabbi's teach that the letters we translate 'Yahweh' were in fact meant to imitate the act of breathing. On this understanding, we can not say God's name in the way we say any other name. In a sense, God's name is un-sayable. But at the same time, through the act of breathing, saying God's name is the very first thing we do, when we come into the world. Saying God's name will be the very last thing we do when we leave it. We will say God's name repeatedly, frantically, in those times we are lost or excited. And even when we think we don't know who God is, in our darkest moments, we say God's name hundreds of times a day!

I hope how wonderful that possibility is justifies such a long background for such a simple exercise!

For an exploration of the bible passage that this practice is rooted in, go to exercise 15.

(Note: You can find an audio version of this and many other practices at https://faithingproject.com/audio-files-associated-with-publications-of-the-faith-ing-project/)

The Exercise

1. Create a space of quiet and safety for yourself by turning off your phone, making the temperature comfortable. Consider getting yourself a glass of water and turning soft, wordless music on.
2. Place your feet flat on the floor. Inhale, slowly through your nose. Exhale, slowly, through your mouth.
3. Place your hand on your abdomen. Feel your belly rise and fall as you continue with your breaths.
4. Spend as long as you wish simply enjoying the act of calmly breathing.
5. When you are ready, see that the exhale is similar to the first syllable of the translation of God's name "Yah."
6. See the inhale as a related to the second syllable, "Weh."
7. Continue to breathe, seeing each breath as a pronouncement of God's name, a name more intimate than any sounds can be.
8. When you are ready, release your conscious thoughts about saying God's name. Enjoy a time of union.
Throughout your day today, return to your breath. Seeing each breath as a calling out to the creator of the universe.

Exercise 2: Breathing with God

Background

It is written that God breathed into the earth and made the first human. This, perhaps, was how the image of God got into man in the first place: through that breath.

If we believe that God continues to be active in the world today, we might come to view that original act of creation as an ongoing event, not a one-time thing. More to the point: perhaps God breathes into us still.

The Exercise

1. Create a safe and quiet space for yourself. Sit up as straight as you comfortably can. Place your feet flat on the floor.
2. Release your worries and responsibilities for the duration of your practice. Don't worry, they will still be there, waiting for you, when you are done.
3. With your next inhale, experience this as God's breath. Your inhale is God breathing in to you.
4. With your next exhale, experience this as a breathing in to God. Your exhale is God's inhale.
5. Continue your practice in this manner. Breathe with God.
6. As your time nears its end, release this imagery of your breathing. Enjoy a time of silent communion.

As you go about your day, pay attention to your breath. Recognize that God breathes with you.

Exercise 3: Being Filled, Being Emptied

Background:

Consider this a sequel to exercise #2. It builds on the practice of breathing with God, but then asks us to use this breath in a powerful manner. With our exhalations, we breathe out the things we do not need. With our inhalations, we take in the things we do need.

This practice also begins to locate our awareness in our body. This is powerful for a few reasons. First, our bodily sensations do not have a memory. They do not have anticipation of the future. Locating our awareness in the body, therefore, is a powerful way to find ourselves right here, right now.

Secondly, we have a tendency to ignore our bodies. Going through the act of being aware of our bodies is an act of remembering our physicality and loving ourselves.

(Note: You can find an audio version of this and many other practices at https://faithingproject.com/audio-files-associated-with-publications-of-the-faith-ing-project/)

The Exercise

Sit up, straight and comfortable.
2. For the duration of your practice today, release yourself from your commitments. Give yourself permission to engage this practice fully.
3. Take a deep, cleansing inhale. Place your hand on your belly and do your best to feel it move; fill your lungs from the bottom, up.
4. Exhale fully, from the bottom of the lungs through the top.
4. With your next inhale, see that this in-breath is God breathing into you.
5. Exhale, fully.
6. With your next inhale, remind yourself of God's presence, breathing into you.
7. Exhale, again.
8. Inhale God's breath into you.
9. For these next few breaths, we will focus on the exhales. With each breath we will be exhaling tension from our body. Continue to breathe slowly and fully.
10. remember that each inhale comes straight from God as we engage this.
11. Inhale, God's breath.

12. Now, exhale. But with your breath, exhale the tension from your feet and calves. Blow it out through your mouth.

13. As you inhale God's breath, feel it filling your all the way down to your feet.

14. As you exhale, breathe out the stress from your knees and thighs.

15. Inhale a breath straight from God. This breath is what makes you human.

16. Exhale the tension from your lap and buttocks.

17. Inhale God's breath into the space you have made. Feel it travel downward from the lungs to the whole lower half of your body.

18. Exhale the tension from your abdomen and lower back.

19. Feel God breath out, and into you.

20. Exhale the tension from your chest and upper back.

21. Inhale a breath from God. Feel the breath first fill your lungs. Let that divine breath fill up the empty space you have made.

22. Exhale the tension from your neck and shoulders.

23. Inhale and feel God's breath fill you from toes to neck.

24. Exhale the tension from your head. Feel it leave your brow, jaw, and the base of your skull. Exhale this stress with your breath.

25. Now, as we begin to draw this exercise to a close, continue to draw God's breath into the empty space you have created. With this next inhale, feel that this oxygen that is spreading to every inch of you is carrying God's love.

26. Exhale stress and tension.

27. Inhale, and see that God's breath is filling up the empty space within you with the deepest Peace.

28. Exhale your worries and concerns.

29. With this next inhale, bring God's breath into the tips of your fingers and toes. Draw it up to the top of your skull. Feel it in all the places in between. And know that this breath is peace.

Exercise #4: A Split Breath Prayer

Background

There are many words which we might want to fully embrace. Repeating these can be a powerful thing. One of the most powerful ways to do this is to split the phrase in half, and assign each half to a part of the breath.
There might be a phrase you wish to substitute with the one in the exercise below. Please feel free to do this.

The Exercise

1. *Place your feet flat on the floor.*
2. *Breathe a few breaths. Relax.*
3. *With your in-breath, place your hand on your abdomen. Bring your attention to really filling your lungs all the way, starting at the bottom and feeling the movement of your belly.*
4. *Exhale. Say to yourself, "Yes. Yes. Yes."*
5. *Inhale. Say to yourself "Thank you. Thank you. Thank you."*
6. *Continue this pattern for most of your practice today.*
7. *Release these words. Continue your calm and slow breaths. Enjoy a time of union.*

When you can, today, return to this breath practice. "Yes. Yes. Yes." "Thank you. Thank you. Thank you."

Exercises 5-7: A Time for Silence, A Time for Words

Background

There are many ways that words can become a gateway to silence. At it's most fundamental, it is really only the possibility of speaking that gives the possibility of choosing silence any kind of meaning. If we could not speak, then silence would be our default condition.

Additionally, there are some times that we want a moment to reflect on the words we are attempting to internalize. In the first exercise (5) below, you will find that the space is created with the in-breath. If there is a sentence or phrase that seems more relevant to you, by all means, explore this one.

In the second exercise that follows, explore the difference between the in-breath and the out-breath. Some authors describe these breath parts as "Breathing up" and "Breathing Down." or "Breathing in" and "Breathing out." Try each of these on for size.

In exercise 7, here is a thing worth exploring: How much of the empty space should you spend continuing to reflect on your sacred words, and for how much of it should you simply inhabit the silence?

This is particularly true when the sacred words are comprised of a list that you are cycling through. As the sacred words change, they invite a different sort of reflection than repetetion.

The list I am suggesting today comes from Ecclesiastes 3. Unfortunately for most of is, it can be challenging to meditate on these truths with out bringing to mind the old song.

Exercise 5

Find an upright, comfortable position. Place your feet flat on the floor. As best you can, release your worries for the duration of this practice.

2. Find your breath. You may wish to consciously slow it. Perhaps, today, you will simply observe it where it is.

3. With your next inhalation, experience the breath as cleansing. It is creating an open space within.

4. With the next exhale, say to yourself– out loud if you can– "God is Love."

5. Let your next inhale create an empty space. Sit in the aftermath of that thought: "God is Love."

6. With your next exhale, think again, "God is Love."

7. With your next exhale, enjoy the silence and emptiness.

8. Continue this pattern, for most of the time you have remaining: 'God is Love' with the inhale; empty openness with the exhale.

9. As your time nears it's completion, let go of the mantra. Widen your time of emptiness to both parts of the breath.

Through out your day today, experience the reality of 'God is Love.' And then, try to live in the space of quiet which transcends even those words.

Exercise 6

Sit as straight as you comfortably can. Breathe for a few minutes and give yourself permission to relax.

2. With your next inhalation, think, "God is Love."

3. Breathe out your thoughts, words and emotions. Use your out-breath to cleanse yourself of everything but the silence.

4. With your next inhalation, again, think "God is Love."

5. As you breathe out, release even your reflections on those 3 words. Exhale your thoughts about this sacred phrase.

6. Continue this pattern for the majority of the time you have given to your spiritual practice today.

7. As you approach the end of the time, release your sacred phrase. Use this time to enjoy wordless communion. Or discuss with God what you learned today. Or simply have a conversation with God about where you are and how things are going.

Exercise 7

1. *Find your center: place your feet on the floor and relax.*
2. *Inhale. Say to yourself "There is a time to be born."*
3. *Exhale.*
4. *Inhale. Say to yourself "There is a time to die."*
5. *Exhale.*
6. *Inhale. Say to yourself, "There is a time to plant."*
7. *Exhale.*
8. *Inhale. Say to yourself "There is a time to kill."*
9. *Exhale.*
10. *Inhale. Say to yourself, "There is a time to heal."*
11. *Exhale.*
12. *Inhale. Say to yourself, "There is a time to tear down."*
13. *Exhale.*
14. *Inhale. Say to yourself, "There is a time to build."*
15. *Exhale.*
16. *Inhale. Say to yourself "There is a time to weep."*
17. *Exhale.*
18. *Inhale. Say to yourself "There is a time to laugh."*
19. *Exhale.*
20. *Inhale. Say to yourself, "There is a time to mourn."*
21. *Exhale.*
22. *Inhale. Say to yourself, "There is a time to dance."*
23. *Exhale.*
24. *Inhale. Say to yourself, "There is a time to scatter stones."*
25. *Exhale.*
26. *Inhale. Say to yourself, "There is a time to gather stones."*

27. Exhale.
28. Inhale. Say to yourself, "There is a time to embrace."
29. Exhale.
30. Inhale. Say to yourself, "There is a time to refrain from embracing."
31. Exhale.
32. Inhale. Say to yourself, "There is a time to search."
33. Exhale.
34. Inhale. Say to yourself, "There is a time to give up."
35. Exhale.
36. Inhale. Say to yourself, "There is a time to keep."
37. Exhale.
38. Inhale. Say to yourself, "There is a time to throw away."
39. Exhale.
40. Inhale. Say to yourself "There is a time to tear."
41. Exhale.
42. Inhale. Say to yourself, "There is a time to mend."
43. Exhale.
44. Inhale. Say to yourself "There is a time to be silent."
45. Exhale.
46. Inhale. Say to yourself, "There is a time to speak."
47. Exhale.
48. Inhale. Say to yourself, "There is a time to love."
49. Exhale.
50. Inhale. Say to yourself, "There is a time to hate."
51. Exhale.
52. Inhale. Say to yourself "There is a time for war."
53. Exhale.
54. Inhale. Say to yourself "There is a time for peace."
55. As you release the individual words, look back on how you felt about each of these. Are there any that you struggle with? Any that come easy?

You might, as you go about your day, assign the various joys and challenges of your life a part from this poem. When entering into a conflict, you could think, for example "This is a time for war." When tempted to say something unwise, you might tell yourself, "This is a time for silence."

Exercise 8 and 9: 3-Part Cycles

Background

A certain phrase paired with an exhale has a slightly different feel than that same phrase paired with an inhale. When we have a 3 phrase cycle, one approach is to simply rotate through all 3 sentences. The result of this is that each phrase gets connected to both inhales and exhales. We can experience, therefore, what those phrases are like.

In the exercises that follow, I have chosen two of my favorite 3-sentence cycles. They are rather Christo-centric. You can, of course, replace them with something more to your liking.

In exercise 8 we focus on the two obvious portions of the breath: The inhale and the exhale. But breath does not have to be a 2-part process. In exercise 9 We can create a 3-count in our breath by pausing for a moment; holding the breath as we consider a phrase.

Holding the breath is an interesting thing. It creates, in me, a distant and deeply submerged sort-of terror. Simultaneously, it is also like a micro-fast. Breathing, like eating, is a requirement. To abstain for a time from either one is to confront our physical limitations and our animal nature.

I suspect that some of this emotional intensity rubs itself off on to the feelings associated with the phrases.

Exercise 8

1. *Place your feet flat on the floor.*
2. *Breathe a cleansing breath.*
3. *With your next inhale, say "Christ was born"*
4. *With your next exhale, "Christ has died."*
5. *With your next inhale, "Christ will come again."*
6. *Continue this pattern, working your way through the entire cycle: Christ was born/ Christ has died/ Christ will come again.*
7. *When you are ready, release the phrases.*
8. *Wordlessly, enjoy some time with God.*

Spend some time, when your practice is done, considering the omnipresence of God. God is here and not here; present and not-yet.

Exercise 9

1. *Find a bit of calm. Place your feet flat on the floor. Breathe slowly.*
2. *With your next inhale, think "Here I am, God."*
3. *As you exhale, think, "Here you are God."*
4. *Holding your breath, think, "Here we are, together."*
5. *Repeat the process: With the inhale, "Here I am God." With the exhale: "Here you are God." Holding the Breath, "Here we are, together."*
6. *Give most of the time in your practice today to these 3 steps.*
7. *When you are ready, release these words. Resume a normal 2-part breathing pattern without holding the breath.*

Throughout your day, know that you are here, and God is here, and you are here, together.

Exercise 10: Mirroring

Background

God knows everything about you. And God loves you, thoroughly, utterly and irrevocably. For the duration of today's practice, please release your feelings and fears about God being angry about who you are or what you have done. While those feelings may be rooted in reality they will not serve you in this practice, because whatever else God feels toward you, God's love is not deniable or negotiable.

Today's practice is inspired by the work of Richard Rohr and others who would have us contemplate God's loving gaze on every part of us.

In this practice, we will begin by experiencing God's gaze on our physical body. We will then experience God's gaze on our minds, and then in our heart.

After a time of experiencing God gazing down on us, and experiencing ourselves, mirroring this gaze back up on God, we will close by breathing out this accumulated Love on the world around us.

The Exercise

1. *Place your feet flat on the floor. Breathe deeply, filling and emptying the lungs as completely as possible.*

2. Inhale. With your breath, inhale the reality that God is love.

3. With your next exhale, exhale the things you fear about what God might think or believe about you.

4. For as many breaths as you need, feel God's loving gaze falling on your body. Perhaps it begins at your feet and works its way up. Let God's gaze stop in places you feel sore, tight, or hurt.

5. For 3 more breaths, feel God's loving gaze on the whole of your physical body.

6. Now, experience God's gaze on your mind. Let it begin on your thoughts and beliefs. Perhaps you will feel this as God's view resting deeply within your head.

7. God's gaze also lands on your memories. It is a loving and healing gaze. As you continue to breathe deeply, feel God's watching fix some of the brokenness of your past.

8. God's gaze will come down to your feelings. Perhaps you will experience God's gaze on your physical heart as God lovingly beholds the contents of your feelings.

9. Continuing to breathe deeply, for 3 breaths, let God take in the whole of your brain and your heart. Feel loved and healed.

10. As you continue these deep inhales, see that God beholds you. All of you. In every moment. As he is watching you, the whole of, watch God. You have become a sort-of mirror, reflecting that loving gaze back up to God.

11. Luxuriate in this. Take as long as you would like. Continue to be present to deep breaths.

12. Just as a mirror turns back all of the light that is casting on it, you are turning back God's gaze fully. Yet, the mirror grows warm. It keeps some of the heat where it is. Let yourself grow warm with God's love.

13. As this heat increases, consider those you love the most. And breathe out your love on them.

14. Continuing to breathe deeply, widen the circle of those you are breathing out love on. Include casual friends.

15. Inhaling, and exhaling, recieving God's love, you can know breathe your love on the whole of the human race.

Exercises 11 and 12: Be Still and Know

Background

The truth? I resisted this one for a while. One minor problem was that it most naturally lead itself to just a few seconds, and I am more interested in practices which lend themselves to twenty minutes or half an hour. But the bigger problem was that it seemed… kind of cute and precious. If spiritual practices had a personality, this one would have seemed very self-satisfied to me. Then? Then I tried it anyway. And I quite like it.

I have provided several different forms of this exercise. The first is the most common. This takes a matter of seconds. Perhaps you will find it useful to use it as a breath prayer as you go about your day. The latter forms are ones which might be more reasonably used through an exercise.

Exercise 11

1. *Place your feet flat on the floor.*
2. *Breathe.*
3. *Think– or say– "Be still, and know that I am God."*
4. *Breathe.*
5. *Think– or say– "Be still and know that I am."*
6. *Breathe.*
7. *Think– or say– "Be still and know"*
8. *Breathe.*
9. *Think– of say– "Be still."*
10. *Breathe.*
11. *Think– or say– "Be."*
12. *Breathe.*

Exercise 12

Place your feet flat on the floor.

2. Breathe.

3. Think– or say– "Be still, and know that I am God."

4. Breathe.

(Repeat this process 3 times.)

5. Think– or say– "Be still and know that I am."

6. Breathe.

(Repeat this process 3 times.)

7. Think– or say– "Be still and know"

8. Breathe.

(Repeat this process 3 times.)

9. Think– of say– "Be still."

10. Breathe.

(Repeat this process 3 times.)

11. Think– or say– "Be."

(Repeat this process 3 times.)

12. Take 3 cleansing Breaths.

Exercises 13 and 14: Gratitude and Loving-Kindness

Background

There is a Buddhist tradition of a loving-kindness meditation. The exercises below are two versions recently practiced in The Faith-ing Project's Thanksgiving Campaign. The first more closely aligns with the Buddhist tradition. The second reworks some of the Buddhist Concepts with a Christian, Gallic framework.

Exercise 13

Create a calm, and quiet space; turn off your phone and do your best to assure yourself of uninterrupted time.

2. For the duration of this exercise, give yourself permission to be free of the duties and obligations that you normally submit yourself to.

3. For a minute or two, simply breathe: in through the nose, and out through the mouth,

4. Think of a person you feel gratitude for. (Choose, more or less randomly, a single person to focus on. Don't worry, you will have an opportunity to focus on others shortly.)

5. Inhale and bring their appearance to your mind. Try and hear their voice, and even smell their unique smell. Feel, as best you can, their presence. Exhale.

6. For the duration of a breath, allow yourself to experience whatever feelings this person stirs within you at this moment.

7. With your next inhale, think to this person 'May you be free from suffering.'

8. Exhale.

9. With your next inhale, think to this person 'May you be healthy.'

10. Exhale.

11. With your next inhale, think 'May you be happy.'

12. Exhale.

13. With your next inhale, think 'May you find peace and joy.'

14. Exhale.

15. For the next breath, rejoice in the thought that your friend would be experiencing all these.

16. If there is more time you had set aside for your spiritual practice, you might move on to another person you feel grateful for. If you are having trouble choosing, consider these questions:

Who are you grateful for in your home? Who are you grateful for in your school or workplace? Who are you thankful for in your social circles? Who are you thankful for from your past? Who are you thankful for in your present? Are there people who took on a role of parent, sibling, boss, coworker, lover, friend, coach, leader, follower that you are thankful for? People who shaped you personally, professionally, or spiritually?

Whoever you choose, the phrases to focus on are these:

May you be free from suffering.

May you be healthy.

May you be happy.

May you find peace and joy.

17. When you are ready to conclude today's practice, take a single, cleansing breath.

18. Now, with your inhale, think this for yourself: May I be free from suffering.

19. Exhale.

20. With your inhale: May I be healthy.

21. Exhale.

22. With your inhale: May I be happy.

23. Exhale.

24. Inhale, think: May I find peace and joy.

Exercise 14

Create a calm, and quiet space; turn off your phone and do your best to assure yourself of uninterupted time.

2. For the duration of this exercise, give yourself permission to be free of the duties and obligations that you normally submit yourself to.

3. For a minute or two, simply breathe: in through the nose, and out through the mouth,

4. Think of a person you feel gratitude for. (Choose, more or less randomly, a single person to focus on. Don't worry, you will have an opportunity to focus on others shortly.)

5. Inhale and bring their appearance to your mind. Try and hear their voice, and even smell their unique smell. Feel, as best you can, their presence. Exhale.

6. For the duration of a breath, allow yourself to experience whatever feelings this person stirs within you at this moment.

7. With your next inhale, think to this person 'May the road rise up to meat you.'

8. Exhale.

9. With your next inhale, think to this person 'May the wind be always at your back.'

10. Exhale.

11. With your next inhale, think 'May the sun shine warm on your face.'

12. Exhale.

13. With your next inhale, think 'May the rains fall softly on your fields'

14. Exhale.

15. With the next inhale, think 'May God hold you in the palm of his hand.'

15. For the next breath, rejoice in the thought that your friend would be experiencing all these.

16. If there is more time you had set aside for your spiritual practice, you might move on to another person you feel grateful for. If you are having trouble choosing, consider these questions:

Who are you grateful for in your home? Who are you grateful for in your school or workplace? Who are you thankful for in your social circles? Who are you thankful for from your past? Who are you thankful for in your present? Are there people who took on a role of parent, sibling, boss, coworker, lover, friend, coach, leader, follower that you are thankful for? People who shaped you personally, professionally, or spiritually?

Whoever you choose, the phrases to focus on are these:

May the road rise up to meet you.

May the wind be always at your back.

May the sun shine warm upon your face;

the rains fall soft upon your fields,

may God hold you in the palm of His hand.

17. When you are ready to conclude today's practice, take a single, cleansing breath.

18. Now, with your inhale, think this for yourself: May the roads rise up to meet me..

19. Exhale.

20. With your inhale: May the winds always be at my back.

21. Exhale.

22. With your inhale: May the sun shine warm upon my face.

23. Exhale.

24. Inhale, think: May the rains fall soft upon my fields.

25. Exhale.

26 Inhale, think, 'May God hold me in the palm of his hand.'

Exercise 15: Tonglen

Background

We spend so much energy running away from negative emotions.
In some ways, they are like a tiny dog chasing an enormous truck. Meditation is when we wonder, "Just what is that dog ever going to do if it catches that truck?" And we stop running from it.

Today's exercise: Buddhist *Tonglen* goes a step beyond merely accepting the inevitability of unpleasantness. In some sense we master it, as we seek it out in others.

This exercise is going to ask you to think about the suffering of someone else. If nothing immediately comes to mind, here are a few things to consider:

A) Can you take on the suffering of someone who opposes you, or who you have difficulty liking?

B) Can you take on the suffering of all those who experience a similar issue to one you struggle with?

The Exercise

The Exercise

1) Place your feet flat on the floor. Breathe slowly through your nose and out through your mouth. Fill you diaphragm with your in-breaths. It can be helpful to place the hand on the abdomen as you do this, to feel its movement.

2) When you are ready to begin this practice in earnest, Breathe in feelings of heaviness, claustrophobia, pain, and hurt. Do not assign this to any experience yet.

3) Breathe out positivity, light, and joy.

4) With your next in-breath, experience the unpleasantness as entering into you through all the pores of your body. Feel it come along with your breath and travel within.

5) When you exude positivity, feel this emenating from your pores, as well as you breath. Envision this goodness going out into the world.

6) Continue this process for a while,.

7) When you are ready, apply your imagination to the experience you have chosen. Take the pain and hurt from the person or group into yourself. Take it through the breath and through the body.

8) Exhale whatever relief you feel is best: Kindness, light and joy.

9) Continue to inhale their pain. Exhale relief.

10) As your practice draws to a close, widen your compassion. If you can, take on the pain in a more intense manner, or feel it coming into you from a wider circle.

11) Continue to exhale love to this widened, deepened circle.

12) When you are ready to release your days practice, spend some time continuing to breathe. Consider what the experience was like of feeling their pain.

Exercise 16 and 17: A Lectio Divina Approach to Exploring God's Breath and name

Background:

These exercises are not breath prayers. They do give us an opportunity to explore the bible passages which some of these passages are rooted in.

The method we will use for these deep dives is *Lectio Divina*. *Lectio* is a centuries-old approach to reading. There are many different ways to approach this. We will try two different approaches to Lectio for the two different bible passages that were alluded to in earlier exercises.

Exercise 16: *Lectio Divina*

1. *Prepare the passage to be read. Open a paper bible to Genesis, Chapter 2. Or open a bible website (such as biblegateway.com) and search the second chapter of Genesis.*
2. *Spend a few minutes breathing and releasing your worries.*
3. *As best you can, with your exhalations, let go of your preconceptions and assumptions of what you are about to read. With each out breath, let go of more of the things you think you know about the reading. Do your best to see these assumptions dissipating into the air.*
4. *When you feel that you have reached a state of beginner's mind, read Genesis Chapter 2 all the way through. On this first reading, just try and get a sense about the big picture.*
5. *When you finish reading through, give yourself some time to breathe.*
6. *Reread the passage. Pay attention to the passages which bring about a reaction in you. Where do you feel stirred?*
7. *Read the passage at least one more time. This time, try and find a specific phrase. Ideally, it should not be more than 5 words long. At most, it should not be more than 10 words long. If you get to the end of the passage and have not found anything, that is ok. Read the passage– or at least a portion of the passage– one last time to select your sacred words.*
8. *Say your words out loud. You might wish to assign one half of the phrase to your inhale, and one half of the phrase to your exhale.*

9. *Spend a good portion of the time repeating your sacred phrase. Leave yourself access to the source material, so you can remind yourself of the wording if you get off track.*
10. *When you are ready, release your sacred words. Sit in wordless union.*

Exercise 17: A second approach to *Lectio*

1. Using a paper bible or an online resource such as Biblegateway.com, prepare Exodus, chapter 3 to be read.
2. Place your feet flat on the ground.
3. Breathe calmly.
4. Speak to God about the names that you and others have for him, Put words to what you know about the word "LORD" and what you remember about the story where Moses encounters the burning bush.
5. Take a few more cleansing breaths.
6. Read the passage that you have selected all the way through.
7. Read the passage again. This time, be on the lookout for words, phrases, and sentences that connect with you. Perhaps it relates to the thoughts and feelings you expressed to God a few minutes ago.
8. Read the passage a third time. This time through, try to hone in on the sentence you will be using in your practice.
9. If you are not yet committed to a certain phrase, read the passage one more time.
10. Choose a phrase of 2-10 words.
11. Repeat your phrase with each breath. You might assign the first half of the phrase to the inhale, and the second half of the phrase to an exhalation.
12. Let this breathing and recitation occupy at least a third of the time you have set aside for your practice today.
13. When you are ready, release this phrase.
14. Discuss the things you experienced today with God.

Section 2: There is Breathing. Is it me?

I had the good fortune to grow up near Disneyland. Out of this crazy pandemonium of rides, lines, and concessions, there is one attraction in particular that sticks out in my mind.

From the outside, there was nothing particularly impressive about it. It was not a high profile ride. It wasn't inspired by a movie, it wasn't a roller coaster, it wasn't built on cutting edge technology, even in the late 70's.

This ride, whose name I could not even tell you, consisted of fake cars on a track. I remember being 8 or 9 and looking with such sober intensity at the small steering wheel on the left hand side. I was quite surprised when I was allowed to sit there. I knew that I was only about half way to driving age. I did my best to be worthy of this great responsibility, steering our little car.

You might not be surprised to learn that the steering wheel was a prop. The belief that I was in charge was a delusion. That car was going to go where it needed to go. My actions were not relevant to what actually happened.

Nonetheless, at the end of the ride, I would have told you that I had been in charge.

There is a part of us. Call it the ego, call it the small self. It believes that it is in charge. of lots of things. The domain I am thinking about today is the breath. It might be easy to agree in the abstract that the ego has lots of delusions of grandeur. But if you are anything like me, the suggestion that we do not control our breath might seem worth pushing back at.

There are good reasons to suppose that we are in charge of the breath. For example, when it seems like I am thinking "Slow your breath down." it seems like I slow my breath down. That is no small thing. This alone makes it appear an open-and-shut case. Who is in charge of my breath? I am.

But one thing worth noticing about this phenomenon is that we couldn't actually explain how it happens. If a disembodied spirit said, "O.K., but how did you slow your breath down?" it would be impossible to explain what we actually did. The most we could say is that we thought and it happened.

Equally significantly, if the disembodied spirit questioned further, it might ask us what happens when we stop thinking about our breathing. If the breath was a thing that we did, if the breath was the charge of the ego, we might expect that when we stop thinking about it, then we stopped breathing. But of course, this is not what happens.

There is a growing body of research in neuroscience which supports the premise that our ego is applying it's narrative after the fact. Our body is doing the things it does.

For all these reasons, it seems like the most we can say is that there are two things that occur together: when we slow our breathing down, we think "Slow your breath down." But does the thought cause the body change? Regardless of whether it does or does not, the ego, the small self, forever eager to take credit for the many things which are beyond it, would surely claim credit for it.

The ego is so much like my 8 year old self. It takes itself so seriously. It is so sure that it has this important job to do. But if I had stopped steering? The car would still turn where it needed to turn. And when we do not tell the body to breathe, it continues to breathe.

The mystic path confronts us with the reality that the boundaries between ourselves, God, and the rest of the universe are much more permeable than they first appear. It is possible that these boundaries exist only in our minds.

Perhaps it is not that I am choosing to breathe. Maybe the universe is breathing me.

The preceding exercises take on a whole new aspect when they are engaged with this mindset. It is worthwhile to wrestle with this possibility: *the universe is breathing me!* And then go back to the first exercise, and find what new treasures await.

There are also some exercises which are quite specific to this way of embracing the universe. The final exercises in this book will view the breath as an event which does not originate in the self at all.

Background

If you wanted to divide up all the spiritual exercises, all the contemplations, all the ways of approaching of mindfulness that have ever been, you could find one convenient dividing line around what they do with the breath.

Many practices begin by asking us to take charge of the breath. Generally speaking, these practices encourage us to slow down our breathing. There are lots of reasons that this is a good idea.

As discussed above, it may not be the most accurate picture of the way things work though.

The other category of practices asks us to simply observe the breath.

The act of simply tuning into the breath can be so much more difficult than it sounds. It is easy to overthink the direction, "Tune into your breath without changing it." Generally speaking, holding this instruction to tightly will lead to struggles. In trying to be too literal we tend to unleash a series of questions and doubts.

As with so many things, entering these exercises in a light hearted manner is wise. If we accept that we will not be perfect at it, we will be able to observe our breath much more effectively.

Exercise 18: Observing the breath

1. Create a safe, quiet space.
2. Sit in a comfortable, upright manner if you are able.
3. Tune in to your breath. Do your best to accept it without changing it.
4. Note whether you are using the mouth, nose, or both.
5. Become aware of specifically where you feel the breath entering the nose or mouth. How does it feel there? What is the temperature?
6. Note the temperature as it comes in.
7. Extend this awareness of the feeling and temperature as the breath leaves you.
8. Where does the breath end in your body? Does your abdomen move? Your chest?
9. When you are ready, increasingly bring yourself into this particular breath. The one you feel right now. This breath, now is the only breath you can ever change. It is wholly unique among all the breaths you will ever feel. Greet each breath. Find its uniqueness.
10. Welcome the special breaths that follow in the same way. Sit in this awareness for most of the time you have devoted to your practice today.
11. When you are ready, return to your everyday life. But know that you can welcome each breath throughout your day.

Background

Thinkers such as Ken Wilber have observed that it is somewhat arbitrary, the ways that we put importance on a single individual. We are made of millions of cells. The cells are arranged in tissues, the tissues are arranged in organs. The organs are arranged in organ systems. The organ systems are arranged in organisms. The organisms are arranged in communities. The communities are arranged in ecosystems. All the ecosystems, when taken together, form the biosphere.

We have consciousness of ourselves as individuals, of course. But this seems like a small reason to put so much of our attention to one middle-level of this arrangement. There is something to be said for the idea that the consciousness we think is running the show is in fact just giving us a report of the things that are already happening.

If you can do the following practice in the presence of a plant, or better yet a tree, that is a definite plus.

Exercise 19: Give and Take

1. Find a comfortable position. Release your worries and expectations. Place your phone on silent mode.

2. Breathe in, through the nose if you can.

3. Breathe out, through the mouth.

4. Try to breathe in more deeply. Place your hand on your abdomen and feel it move.

5. Exhale again.

6. Take one last inhale, before we move into the next step. Can you make it your deepest?

7. Fully exhale.

8. Spend a moment considering a plant or tree. Behold and love it. Consider the individuality of this one specific plant. See it's leaves and branches. Imagine the roots of the thing. Allow your thoughts or eyes to really linger on this friend.

9. With your next inhale, breathe in. Recognize that some of the very air you breathed might have been made from that plant.

10. With your next exhale, breathe the air out knowing this is what the plant will need. It will inhale the carbon dioxide of your breath.

11. Take two more deep breaths, connecting with the plant in this relationship of oxygen and carbon dioxide.

12. When you are ready, try to erase the boundaries between yourself and the plant. Can you imagine a level upon which you and the plant are not two seperate individuals but one common entity? Experience a sense of oneness with the tree or plant. It is giving you what you need. You are giving it what it needs.

13. Linger on this experience for as long as you need or want to.

14. Widen this circle in your mind. See yourself and this tree as a part of all plant-animals and animals within your area. (perhaps this area is about the size of a city block.) First, sit with the idea that they are in a perfect, reciprocal cycle of oxygen and carbon dioxide.

15. The gasses, in a way, are just a metaphor for so much more. Sit in your place in this system. Make it larger, in your mind, if you wish. First, broaden the meaning of relationship, knowing (but don't bother listing) that we get more than just oxygen. Then, broaden the size of the network.

16. When you have made this network as broad, and deep as your mind will allow, sit with it. In some important sense, all the living creatures in your mind, all the plants and the animals, they are one.

16. If you would like, consider whether God is present within the animals or plants in this relationship. Is God above them? Or the movement of the matter and energy between them? Both? Neither?

17. Hold this web of connection: you, other animals, plants, trees, God in your mind. Take as long as you would like to sit as one part of this network of relationships.

18. When you are ready, return in your mind to just you and the plant you begin with. Consider the differences between yourself and the plant. Try and hold to the idea that you are still one. But the plant has specialties. So do you. The organism that is formed between the two of you is greater than the sum of your parts. Think about the ways that you and the plant are such a good pair.

19. When you are ready to dismiss this practice, thank the plant and move into your day, knowing that you can bring your mind back to your place in this tremendous network of beings.

Exercise 20: Part of a System

1. *Find a relaxed position. Generally speaking, this will be a seated position with feet flat on the floor and spine as straight as is comfortable.*
2. *Notice your breath. Allow yourself to be aware of it with out seeking to change it.*
3. *Feel the inhale: notice where the breath comes in on the nostrils or mouth. Observe the flow of air down the throat and into the belly.*
4. *Feel the exhale. Notice the difference in the temperature and moisture of the air as it leaves the body.*
5. *Continue this for at least three more breaths. Continue longer if that feels right.*
6. *As you continue to observe this process, recall that a story goes that God reached down and breathed into a handfull of Earth. After that breath, there was Adam.*
7. *Observe the exhale.*
8. *Continue this for two more breaths: God-in-the-universe is breathing you.*
9. *Open your heart and mind to the awareness that other people and animals in your area (perhaps your family in other bedrooms, or the other occupants of the building you are in) are breathing, too; God-in-the-universe is breathing them.*
10. *As you complete a second and third breathe with this awareness, continue to observe this breath being breathed in you.*
11. *Open your mind and heart to the plants and even microscopic organisms all around you. Some living things inhale oxygen and exhale carbon dioxide. Others do the reverse. See the world breathing in all these creatures.*

12. *Sit in this flow and connection for as long as you would like.*
13. *Can you widen this network of connections? Can you make it geographically larger? Can you expand the nature of the interconnections.*
14. *When you are ready, return to your everyday world. Hold on to the connections between the rest of the world that were deepened here.*

Afterword

There are so many possible next steps for you.

You might build your spiritual practice from the 16 exercises that were included in this ebook. You might continue to leverage the resources the *Faith-ing Projects* have made available to you. You also might decide that you are ready to take a deeper dive within a specific tradition or type of practice.

Much more important than which of the above options you choose is the simple fact of doing something. Change is possible. Contemplation has lots to offer you. I hope that you are ready.

Wishing you peace on the journey,

Jeff

Printed in Great Britain
by Amazon